UNPLUG

BREATHE

CREATE

A MONTH OF IGNITING YOUR CREATIVITY THROUGH MEDITATION

Unplug Breathe Create: A Month of Igniting Your Creativity Through Meditation is a work of my own creation.

Cover, Book Design, and Layout by megs thompson, megswrites llc
www.megswrites.com

www.inomniaparatuspublishing.com

"THE OBJECT ISN'T TO MAKE ART IT'S TO BE IN THAT WONDERFUL STATE WHICH MAKES ART INEVITABLE."

—ROBERT HENRI

This journal is part of the
UNPLUG BREATHE CREATE
series & designed to be used
alongside a bespoke guided
meditation.

Download this month's meditation
using the QR code below:

HOW TO BEST USE THIS JOURNAL & MEDITATION

UNPLUG

The first step to reconnecting with ourselves as creative beings is to unplug & disconnect even temporarily from the countless electronic tethers that keep us firmly held in the world of shoulds & must's.

BREATHE

Take a few deep breaths, paying close attention to the way oxygen moves through your mouth & nose, filling your lungs & reawakening the creative genius locked safely within you, exhaling any fears, hesitations, or doubts that may filter your magic.

CREATE

Release your desire to control, plan & perfect every step & movement you make. Embrace the often wild, messy & chaotic magic that comes with allowing your inner creative to explore & play. Prepare yourself to experience fulfillment & satisfaction in new & creative ways.

DAILY ROUTINE

While moving through your day, begin implementing the use of affirmations. Both habits & beliefs are formed & strengthened through consistent repetition & before you know it your thoughts will become truths.

Included below are powerful affirmations that when paired with your daily tasks & activities, will empower you through this month of finding & claiming your own creative space.

I recommend repeating one or more of these affirmations aloud anytime you find yourself in front of a mirror, washing your hands, or refilling your beverage of choice.

I AM A POWERFULLY CREATIVE BEING.

I AM WORTHY OF SPENDING TIME EXPLORING MY CREATIVE SPIRIT.

MY LIFE IS MEANT TO BE ENJOYED.

30-DAY ENERGY TRACKER

When you've completed your daily meditation, make note of a single word or phrase that best describes your energy level in that moment.

Day 1	Day 2	Day 3	Day 4	Day 5
Day 6	Day 7	Day 8	Day 9	Day 10
Day 11	Day 12	Day 13	Day 14	Day 15
Day 16	Day 17	Day 18	Day 19	Day 20
Day 21	Day 22	Day 23	Day 24	Day 25
Day 26	Day 27	Day 28	Day 29	Day 30

DAY 1

During meditation you visualized a board covered with small pieces of paper. Spend a few minutes journaling what tasks & obligations you saw on those papers?

_____

_____

_____

_____

_____

_____

_____

_____

_____

_____

_____

_____

_____

_____

_____

ON A SCALE OF 1-5 WHAT'S YOUR
CURRENT CREATIVITY LEVEL?

DAY 2

Looking back at your journaling from yesterday, do you feel confident in releasing your focus on these obligations & instead directing your attention toward your creative spirit?

ON A SCALE OF 1-5 WHAT'S YOUR
CURRENT CREATIVITY LEVEL?

DAY 3

In as much detail as possible, describe what your creative space looks like, feels like, smells like, sounds like. Where is it located? Is this a place you've visited before? What is it about this space that invites you to reconnect with your creative spirit?

ON A SCALE OF 1-5 WHAT'S YOUR
CURRENT CREATIVITY LEVEL?

DAY 4

Spend a few moments reflecting on when in your life you feel the most creative? Is this within your personal or professional life? How often are you able to enjoy this time?

ON A SCALE OF 1-5 WHAT'S YOUR CURRENT CREATIVITY LEVEL?

DAY 5

When was the last time you felt creative? Where were
you? What were you doing? Who were you with? How
can you bring more of this into your daily life?

ON A SCALE OF 1-5 WHAT'S YOUR
CURRENT CREATIVITY LEVEL?

DAY 6

What resistance or fears do you feel around the idea of sharing your creativity with others? Are these feelings based in past experiences or assumptions?

ON A SCALE OF 1-5 WHAT'S YOUR
CURRENT CREATIVITY LEVEL?

DAY 7

What are your favorite forms of creative expression?
This may be words, music, paint, food, dance, clay,
wood, steel, yarn, etc. When was the last time you
took an afternoon to enjoy this creative outlet?

ON A SCALE OF 1-5 WHAT'S YOUR
CURRENT CREATIVITY LEVEL?

DAY 8

How did you most enjoy expressing yourself creatively as a child? Is that something you might still enjoy today?

ON A SCALE OF 1-5 WHAT'S YOUR
CURRENT CREATIVITY LEVEL?

DAY 9

Close your eyes. Take 3 deep breaths & ask yourself, how do I want to explore my creativity today? What answer do you receive? How comfortable are you with trusting your intuition to guide your creativity?

ON A SCALE OF 1-5 WHAT'S YOUR
CURRENT CREATIVITY LEVEL?

DAY 10

When was the last time you felt stuck or stifled in regard to your creative expression? What was stopping you? Was it an outside force, perceived judgement from others, or your own limiting beliefs?

ON A SCALE OF 1-5 WHAT'S YOUR
CURRENT CREATIVITY LEVEL?

DAY 11

What is one task that you complete every day. This may be something mundane, administrative & without much sparkle. How can you approach this task from a more creative standpoint?

_____

_____

_____

_____

_____

_____

_____

_____

_____

_____

_____

_____

_____

_____

_____

_____

ON A SCALE OF 1-5 WHAT'S YOUR
CURRENT CREATIVITY LEVEL?

DAY 12

How often do you allow yourself to embrace your own creativity? What's holding you back from prioritizing this time? As with any habit or skill, consistent repetition strengthens & solidifies your confidence as a creative being. Are you able to set aside 10, 20, or even 30 minutes each day to explore your creativity?

ON A SCALE OF 1-5 WHAT'S YOUR
CURRENT CREATIVITY LEVEL?

DAY 13

What lights you up? What topics or areas in life are you most passionate about? How do you currently use your creativity in these areas? How might you be able to better tap into your creativity?

_____

_____

_____

_____

_____

_____

_____

_____

_____

_____

_____

_____

_____

_____

_____

_____

ON A SCALE OF 1-5 WHAT'S YOUR
CURRENT CREATIVITY LEVEL?

DAY 14

Spend a few moments visualizing your highest most authentic self. This is the greatest version of yourself that you can imagine. How do you feel? How do you spend your time? Who do you surround yourself with?

_____

_____

_____

_____

_____

_____

_____

_____

_____

_____

_____

_____

_____

_____

_____

_____

ON A SCALE OF 1-5 WHAT'S YOUR
CURRENT CREATIVITY LEVEL?

DAY 15

What are 5 traits that set you apart from others? Think of things that make you the unique individual you are. How do these attributes serve you? How do they limit you?

ON A SCALE OF 1-5 WHAT'S YOUR
CURRENT CREATIVITY LEVEL?

DAY 16

What are 3 aspects of your daily life that bring you the most joy. How might you increase the creativity associated with these three tasks/situations/experiences?

ON A SCALE OF 1-5 WHAT'S YOUR
CURRENT CREATIVITY LEVEL?

DAY 17

If you were to write a short story with yourself as the main character, where would the story take place? Would you exist as you do now, or would you take a different form?

ON A SCALE OF 1-5 WHAT'S YOUR
CURRENT CREATIVITY LEVEL?

DAY 18

Write a short love letter or note to your ideal creative space, or favorite creative tool/material.

ON A SCALE OF 1-5 WHAT'S YOUR
CURRENT CREATIVITY LEVEL?

DAY 19

What place or space gives you the most peace & clarity? Describe this place or space using all of your senses, in as much detail as possible.

ON A SCALE OF 1-5 WHAT'S YOUR
CURRENT CREATIVITY LEVEL?

DAY 20

What drives you to get up every morning? What is your big 'why?' This may vary personally & professionally, although when your 'why' is aligned with your core values it will often carry over into all areas of your life.

ON A SCALE OF 1-5 WHAT'S YOUR
CURRENT CREATIVITY LEVEL?

DAY 21

Failure is a part of life, it's also part of the creative process. When did you last fail during a creative project? Focus on the fact that while the outcome may have fallen short of your intention, it was temporary & there is no reason to not try again.

_____

_____

_____

_____

_____

_____

_____

_____

_____

_____

_____

_____

_____

_____

....
....
....
_____
_____
....
....
_____
....
....
_____
_____
....
....
_____

ON A SCALE OF 1-5 WHAT'S YOUR CURRENT CREATIVITY LEVEL?

DAY 22

What sounds, smells, colors, temperatures, or environments most ignite your creative confidence? Do you have a specific soundtrack you like to listen to, or a candle you light?

ON A SCALE OF 1-5 WHAT'S YOUR
CURRENT CREATIVITY LEVEL?

DAY 23

Where do you feel the most resistance when it comes to embracing your own creativity? Are these feelings based in past experiences or assumptions?

ON A SCALE OF 1-5 WHAT'S YOUR
CURRENT CREATIVITY LEVEL?

DAY 24

As children, we're naturally curious & willing to try new things, getting creative even when it may be uncomfortable. How can you embrace your childlike curiosity & creativity now?

_____

_____

_____

_____

_____

_____

_____

_____

_____

_____

_____

_____

_____

_____

_____

_____

_____

ON A SCALE OF 1-5 WHAT'S YOUR
CURRENT CREATIVITY LEVEL?

DAY 25

Oftentimes the key to building creative confidence is maintaining a beginner's mindset, remaining open & curious to the countless solutions surrounding us. How can you better embrace a beginners mindset?

ON A SCALE OF 1-5 WHAT'S YOUR
CURRENT CREATIVITY LEVEL?

DAY 26

When do you feel most creatively confident? Where in your body do you feel this? How would you describe this feeling or sensation? How might you be able to weave this into your daily life?

ON A SCALE OF 1-5 WHAT'S YOUR
CURRENT CREATIVITY LEVEL?

DAY 27

Spend a few moments journaling about creative projects, ventures & experiences that you'd like to explore. Make a plan for how you're going to pursue one of these dreams within the next 30 days.

ON A SCALE OF 1-5 WHAT'S YOUR
CURRENT CREATIVITY LEVEL?

DAY 28

When was the last time you created something for fun, without purpose or direction? What did you enjoy most about the process. What hesitations did you experience.

ON A SCALE OF 1-5 WHAT'S YOUR
CURRENT CREATIVITY LEVEL?

DAY 29

What creative gifts do you have to give the world?
Brag!!!

ON A SCALE OF 1-5 WHAT'S YOUR
CURRENT CREATIVITY LEVEL?

DAY 30

What affirmations are you taking with you into the next week, month, year to ignite your creativity?

ON A SCALE OF 1-5 WHAT'S YOUR
CURRENT CREATIVITY LEVEL?

If you already have an
UNPLUG BREATHE CREATE
subscription, keep an eye on your
mailbox for your next delivery.

If you aren't yet a member but
would like to be, or are
interested in gifting a
membership to someone else,
scan the QR code below.